STILL LIFE
WITH
MOTHER
AND
KNIFE

STILL LIFE
WITH
MOTHER
AND
KNIFE

poems

For Andrea
With all best wishes

Chelsea Rathburn

Chelsea Rathburn (signature)

LOUISIANA STATE
UNIVERSITY PRESS
BATON ROUGE

Published with the assistance of the Sea Cliff Fund

Published by Louisiana State University Press
Copyright © 2019 by Chelsea Rathburn
All rights reserved
Manufactured in the United States of America
LSU Press Paperback Original

DESIGNER: Michelle A. Neustrom
TYPEFACE: Sina Nova

LIBRARY OF CONGRESS CATALOGING-IN-PUBLICATION DATA

Names: Rathburn, Chelsea, 1975– author.
Title: Still life with mother and knife : poems / Chelsea Rathburn.
Description: Baton Rouge : Louisiana State University Press, [2019]
Identifiers: LCCN 2018035314 | ISBN 978-0-8071-6974-2 (pbk. : alk. paper) |
    ISBN 978-0-8071-6976-6 (pdf) 978-0-8071-6975-9 (epub)
Classification: LCC PS3618.A86 A6 2019 | DDC 811/.6—dc23
LC record available at https://lccn.loc.gov/2018035314

The paper in this book meets the guidelines for permanence and durability
of the Committee on Production Guidelines for Book Longevity
of the Council on Library Resources. ♾

for Adelyn

[The child] wonders who or what projects him into adversity,
and what can prevent this from happening to him.
Are there benevolent powers in addition to his parents?
Are his parents benevolent powers?

—BRUNO BETTELHEIM, *The Uses of Enchantment*

CONTENTS

STILL LIFE
WITH
MOTHER
AND
KNIFE

Postpartum: A Fairy Tale

The pages of our storybook childhoods were ripped
from the Brothers Grimm, the woods always in shadow,
the apples poisoned, the ladders made of bone,
our mothers telling us early how much they loved
and loathed us: how my aunt had wished to find
my cousin drowned in the washing machine,
while my mother hoped her cat would climb the walls
of my crib and steal my breath. Our longed-for endings
told gleefully and in the passive voice.
Those days were gone, they told us, but we wondered.
If, as Bettelheim writes, the witches and giants
in the brutal fairy tales are really stand-ins
for the parents the child is afraid to fear and love,
what did we make of our mothers' revelations,
which made us the monstrous creatures, changelings left
by trolls? That they could not, or would not, save us.
That we had to learn to walk the woods alone.

I.

Introduction to Captivity

The days we wandered the drugstore aisles,
my cousin and I, counting out coins
for makeup we were too young to wear—
all of them gone, the drugstore too,
and the tropical nursery where
our parents dragged us despite the heat,
and the caged capuchin who sat
scowling in that nursery. While
our parents wove through towering rows
of palms, we crouched beside the cage
to watch the monkey eat the grit
he pulled from his nose. We threw pebbles
into the cage and he ate them, too,
and reached for the pennies I flashed at him.
My cousin waved her lipstick next,
a purple only an eight-year-old
could love, and he scrambled for the tube.
Does a monkey smeared in Frosted Orchid
look that much worse than a child does?
At my cousin's wails, our parents came running
to find the monkey, lips aglow,
shaking a purpled fist in rage
or consolation through the bars.
Gone those lush and potted plants,
gone our burning girlhoods, yearning
to be older, to be prettier,
to be anyone else. It was lucky,
they told us, laughing, he didn't bite.

Introduction to Statistics

Suppose we surprised him coming off the path
into the patch of pines and saw palmettos,
two girls with our child-sized bikes. Suppose
he had a reason to chase us back to the path,
his pale face flushed with—what? Desire? Wrath?
He shouted *Come back* but we fled. Who knows
what he was doing there in the woods. Impose
an innocent narrative and still the math
will come out wrong. There was a flash of skin,
a man in yellow shorts with dark brown curls,
a shout. And in the dream that I'm still in
he stumbles out, a living question mark,
and we are halfway gone. We're only girls
playing in the woods. It's hours before dark.

Introduction to Home Economics

I'm not convinced my mother ever forgave me
for carving, instead of the jack-o-lantern, the hand
she used to steady it in her lap. We sat
on the porch with a kitchen knife, newspapers spread
beneath us. The pumpkin's skin was stubborn, my mother
left-handed. I was six, my mantra *Let me try.*
Then blood and blood and blood. Then tourniquets
of towels and the rush to the E.R.,
my father driving. I stayed behind with a neighbor,
my mother returning with black stitches, her hand
wrapped like a mummy's, to finish the face we'd started.
Each Halloween, she brought it up again,
reminding me what I had done, how I had hurt her,
though she was the one who handed me the knife.

Introduction to Vigilance

When I was six, Alice held metal scissors to my head
and pretended to trim my hair. We were in arts & crafts.
Hearing the cold click, I turned with my own pair of blades.

A cord—waist-length, ice-blond—slipped off her shoulder. Alice cried,
But I was kidding, I wouldn't cut your hair!, and snipped again,
this time in earnest. Teacher scolded: we could have cut ourselves.

Mothers were called. Our hair grew back, although too slowly for
school picture day. And we both loved our indignation, the way
a dog waits hours at the window for a chance to bark.

Alice, my best friend, said the damage I'd inflicted on her
was worse than what I'd suffered, because her hair was prettier.
It's true my mother always botched my bangs. My husband teases

I'm like our dog sometimes, her hackles rise at the slightest threat:
the neighbors, robins in the grass, a cat come for the robins.
Such grievances. And if a man followed you—your younger self—

into a bathroom and unzipped his pants, whom would you tell?
I told Alice alone. She told a friend, who told her mother,
and I was afraid I might be killed but was also relieved.

That year I looked for ways to slip from notice, even my shoulders
curving inward, a posture I would wear for a decade,
vigilant in retreat. Why think of any of this now,

the dog asleep, still facing the window, my husband reading beside me,
always ready to say I'm beautiful? Such a small thing
I was, poised to cut or run, my bangs an injured wobbling line.

Introduction to Gerontology

These were the trappings of old age: pitchers
of sun tea steeping on the patio;
the TV tuned to *General Hospital*
or *Wheel of Fortune;* tall brass ashtrays
by every chair, sentries ready to swallow
another lipstick-smudged Benson & Hedges
at the push of a deco button; a '58
Pontiac Bonneville, impossibly long,
all chrome and fins; and our next-door neighbor's
white silk blouses and pressed white curls, both wilting
only slightly in the heat.
                              Widowed
some twenty years, stepdaughters long estranged,
our neighbor shrank inside her rocking chair
as the days stretched on, an orphan in reverse.
Mrs. Down talked to the soap operas
and game show hosts until the doorbell rang.
Because I had no grandmother to speak of,
I ran across the lawn each afternoon
and rang that doorbell and was let inside,
sitting with her as she smoked furiously
and complained about the weather, the plots,
the TV dinners she picked at, and later,

after her eyes had gone and the Bonneville
was garaged forever, the dinners my mother cooked
and I delivered on a flowered tray,
keeping her company as she ate and smoked
the cigarettes my father bought her. Some nights
I stayed over, and we played Spite & Malice
with two decks of Eastern Airlines cards.
She grumbled curses when I won, which wasn't
often; she shuffled her stacks when I looked down.

I thought old age made everyone angry,
though now I know her rage was hers alone.

I loved her anyway: the downy white hair,
the hump of her back, her tiny bottles of perfume,
how she remembered everything, and told
it all to me—her family's first car,
white gloves and dances, her days as a Matron
in the Order of the Eastern Star. And now
I remember nothing but scraps of stories
and objects, the turquoise of the lounge chair,
the crepe myrtle's bloom. When I was twelve,
she let a nephew talk her into moving
so that she'd "never have to be alone"—

she built two houses side by side upstate
and signed over her power of attorney,
though we didn't know it then. When we visited
that sterile living room, her furniture
looked out of place and her voice had lost its edge.
The emphysema came as no surprise,
but we didn't know she'd died until I tracked
the nephew down. By then, all was sold
or burned, the glittering Eastern Star pins
and paperweights, the dusty-red Pontiac,
the body with its lipstick and its pearls.

Introduction to Thanatology

On her seventh birthday, Alice said
we should try to make ourselves faint.
Her older brother had told her how:

you had to hold your breath while someone
pushed on your chest. When the first girl tried,
nothing happened, so I offered

myself up to their hands, Alice
giving orders at my feet.
On the count of three, I was no longer

at a slumber party but lying still
on a black table in a black room
with, yes, a slice of bright white light.

A stuttering sound, some fractured cry,
filled my ears in a voice that became
my own. And then the worried faces

as I came to, my mouth repeating
what I'd heard, what I thought was a word,
some urgent message from beyond

that no one understood. Alice
had been about to get her mother,
afraid they couldn't call me back

from wherever it was I'd gone,
but now she swore us all to secrecy.
We didn't know that kids could die

from games like this. We didn't know
that kids like us could die. We never
tried again, but I remembered

sometimes how easy it was to slip
free of the body, like stepping from a robe,
and how certain I felt in that black space,

my friends and the darkness calling me.

Introduction to Patriarchy

For a while we found them everywhere we looked,
tucked in our brothers' closets or slipped inside
our fathers' attachés: carousels
of airbrushed women with rumpled curls
wearing sweaters or raincoats or negligees
or nothing but shoes. (Their feet were never bare.)

Bedecked in stockings and heels as tall as stilts,
they seemed as though they always had to grab
ahold of something strong—a doorframe, say,
or a fire hose—or lean across a bed
to keep from toppling. Top-heavy, lips wet,
one arm lifted or crossed, they waited for us.

Side by side, our bodies hairless, all lines
and sharp angles, we studied their proportions.
We read about their favorite centuries
(*The 20th, because women can finally*
pursue their own individuality
and potential!) and ideal men, and memorized

their vague ambitions. Ranking their parts, we fought
over who got to be Miss October
or Miss April when we played—what was the game?
It can't be called dress-up if we undressed.
Instead of doctors or astronauts, we channeled
waitresses in a topless bar. We practiced

carrying trays and looking vacant or surprised.
When our big breaks came, we posed for centerfolds,
eager to please the invisible camera.
We leaned against the wall or dropped to our hands
and knees, our smiles fixed, until our fathers'
voices sent us fumbling for our clothes.

Introduction to Sex Education

Our final project was to paint a face
on a raw egg, nestle it in a cardboard crib,
and carry it for a week. Some girls made lace
pajamas, one fashioned an egg-sized bib,
but this was missing the point, our teacher said:
babies were hell: a never-leaving need,
hungry and squalling, shit-stained, refusing bed.
Our eggs were easy—no diapers, no mouths to feed—
and even so our parenting was lax.
We crammed our progeny in lockers, dropped
them on the bus. We patched their hairline cracks
when we could with Elmer's glue. The worst were swapped.
What had we learned, if we had stopped to think?
To forge Ms. Greene's initials in blue ink.

Introduction to Desire

For years it was the smell of luck—my own,
not my rained-on neighbors': that boiling sludge
men pulled from barrels and spread on ailing roofs.
From blocks away I was lured by scent or the glimpse
from my mother's car window of drums of tar.

The air alive and thrumming, like a bush
in flower throbbing with bees, the heat rose
like a cartoon pie's visible vapors.
And like a cartoon character, I drifted
from the house, pedaling up and down the street

as slowly as I could without falling
because I loved the smell, almost-death,
almost-perfume, dark and vertiginous.
I knew enough to feel slightly ashamed.
What did the roofers think? In high school

I was reformed by the hurricane: a year
of roofing crews on every street at once,
the smell following me, clinging to my clothes
till I was sick, a betrayal I taste
each time I turn down a freshly paved road.

Introduction to Mycology

FOR E.B., KILLED IN A WORKPLACE MASSACRE

Shiitake, velvet foot, hen of the woods,
wood ear, cloud ear, slippery jack, brown wreaths

of Polish borowik dried and hanging
in the stalls of a Kraków market—all these

were years away from the room where I lay
once, studying the contours of your sex

as if it were some subterranean species
I'd never encounter again. Because I hadn't

yet tasted oyster—not even portobello—
when I thought *mushroom,* I meant the common white

or button, the ones my mother bought for salads
or served in butter beside my father's steak.

First taste of love, or toxic look-alike,
there was your stalk and cap, the earth and dark,

our hunger, wonder, and need. Even now,
I can't identify exactly what

we were, or why, some twenty years later,
learning you lay dying—were in fact

already dead, suspended by machines if not
belief—I thought first of your living flesh,

the size and shape of you. My *amanita
phalloides,* that room was to exist forever,

as a field guide or mossy path, even
if as we foraged, we did not once look back.

Introduction to Art History

I. *Fountain,* 1917

In the half-dark we sat, most of us half-
awake as Ms. Bagwell rocked on thin heels,
clicking through slides on an ancient projector,

tracing our progress from the walls of caves
through fertile and faceless Venus of Willendorf
to the ancient Greeks' golden boys and gods.

Having signed up for the gentle Impressionists
whose prints hung on our kitchen calendar,
I suffered through the Rococo and David.

I was suspicious of the French Romantics'
tumult and restraint, the exaggerated tension
in those bodies splayed across battlegrounds

and rafts, and all the women bare-chested
for no apparent reason. But by the spring
I decided I loved it all, even what

I hadn't liked, especially the way
Ms. Bagwell nearly leaped out of her shoes
at her favorite slides, her hands flying, breathless

as she tried to tell us everything she knew
before the bell. Even when I couldn't see
what she saw in a square of flat black paint

or a porcelain urinal, I wanted to,
wanted to be, without embarrassment
or irony, transformed by what I loved.

II. *A Brief History of Women's Art*

This woman artist, who was classically trained,
posed for great men. Her face is in your book.
This woman artist quit when her husband complained.
This one was famous for the lovers she took.
This woman artist married a painter, a genius,
and put aside her work for his career.
This woman artist did not paint with her penis.
This one, if her work had left the domestic sphere,
could have been good. This one married and had
three children and loved them. This woman artist went mad.

III. *The Birth of Venus*

The artists my friends and I imagined
ourselves as we skulked through the halls
of high school, a thrift-store battalion
in our black shirts and mismatched coats,
were nothing like the sculptor I met
in college who paid me eight an hour
to stretch naked on a sunroom couch
and let myself be sketched. Older,
but not by much, she could have stepped
from the frame of a Botticelli—
blonde curls, nearly transparent skin—
but more surprising than her beauty
was how she radiated happiness,
which should have been art's antidote.
And I looked nothing like the women
splayed across *Art through the Ages,*
my body narrow, small-breasted, nothing
like those virgin mothers, bathers,
and concubines, all of them busty
and glowing, all of them inviting
or avoiding the viewer's eye. Who was
to be my model? I who never
knew exactly where to look, or what
to do with all my grief and anger,
or where to put my restless hands.

II.

Incompetent Cervix

The name sounds hopelessly Victorian—
I'd heard the term and thought of dressing gowns,
ruffled and prim, or suitors waving salts
around a lady on a fainting couch,
not this theater, with its cold table,
its pulleys and knives, not this race to sew
me shut before I spill. Not me. Not then.
But in my present tense, invalid, unstable,
incompetent, I catalog my faults
and hopes. I'm but a flimsy, bulging pouch.
Where is the *I* I was a day ago?
Half out of sight, the surgeon tugs and frowns
until I'm corseted. Knotted and braced,
I'm to be sent home to bed, chastened and chaste.

The Stitch

The months she grew inside me, it did too,
pitting and scarring with each early contraction,
grafting itself to the walls it was meant to truss.

In the operating room at seventeen weeks,
the doctor said to think of my uterus

as a drawstring purse, and the stitch in my cervix
the cord that would cinch it closed. *We pull tight
and knot it,* he said, *until you've gone full-term.*

Untie the knot, the stitch slips free. His hands
drew pictures in the air, his voice was warm

and calming, and I imagined soft thread
or filament as thin as spun sugar,
but then he disappeared behind the drape.

At home, before the baby's first flutters
and kicks, I felt the stitch's tug and scrape,

the sharp and constant pinch a reminder
of the danger we'd escaped, the danger I was.
Invasive stranger to whom I was bound,

it doubled me over on stairs and speedbumps
and made cameos in each ultrasound.

For months I worried that the knot would break,
but in the end the stitch, grown part of me,
refused to loosen. So much for slipping free.

The doctor brought a tackle box of clamps
and scissors to the makeshift surgery

and apologized for what he'd do. When the stitch
at last was out, he left it on a tray:
not thread but wire, a thick and mangled ball

we took a picture of, though unsure why,
stubborn stillborn, the tether that bound us all.

Metamorphoses

Like Daphne turned to laurel in the chase,
the thick and pulsing cord that held us close
in utero, once it was clipped and clamped,
changed from a living thing to a dry stump,
gnarled as a root, if a root were tipped in blood.

And the child it had fed now understood
that I was the cause and end of suffering and cried
all hours, she who alone could recognize
me, a stranger to myself, a monster-mother,
but wanted me because she knew no other.

Postpartum: Lullaby

When two-thirty midnight ten

When the baby cries again

When at her breast a parasite

When she is up and down all night

A voice like a wound in her head in her ear

A rational wound calm and clear

By day she whispers promises

By day she smiles and swaddles and kisses

By night beneath a callous moon

When she alone can soothe she croons

aloud aloud the unallowed

I want to blow my brains out now

And still they rock and rock and rock

beside a cold indifferent clock

Not-Child

Not-planned, not-wanted child—no, not a child,
but rogue unruly cells latched briefly where
the doctors said that nothing more could live,
your not-yet-heart complex and primitive,
like one of those strange plants that feed on air—
I'd say your loss was great, your mother wild

with grief, but that's not true. It and I were not.
I thought all mother-love strong as belief
but I held the wanted child I'd earlier fought
to save, and did not give you face or name.
And when the end I knew was coming came,
I stayed in bed ashamed of my relief.

III.

The Corinthian Women

Shall I go in? Shall *I* go in?
We should stop the murder of the children.
—THE CHORUS, Euripides' *Medea,* Tr. Wilner

Say what you like: that we were wretched, weak,
too quick to pity, that we envied her powers,
that the monstrous guilt as much as hers was ours
because we knew and knowing did not speak.
Of course you think you could have spared the child
squirming beneath the blade, destroyed the poison,
somehow suppressed her madness and her reason.
Call us barbaric all, feminine and wild.

Say we'd gone in, say we had stopped the knife
(don't you think that we were desperate for that choice?),
she'd still have had her potions and her fury;
she'd still have found the means to wreck her life.
Our role was fixed: to flank the gates and worry,
to speak behind our masks in a single voice.

Variations on a Theme:
Delacroix's Medea, 1820–1862

I.

In an early sketchbook, she first appears
a passing thought. Penciled beneath an arm's

labeled musculature, this note: *Medea*
kills her 2 children. She mocks the daughters

of Pelias after they butcher their father.
In the margin, the black slash of a sentence

struck through. Delacroix writes in his journal,
March 1824, *Medea engrosses me.*

He is engrossed, of course, by countless others—
Titian and Velázquez, poetry, housemaids,

the nature of art—but there's something in the myth
that tugs, a fascination he never explains,

though his notebooks preserve love letters, ailments,
and records of the cost of pastries and paints.

II.

For years he seeks a way into the work.
He sketches the children sucking at her breasts,

he studies her neck and torso, turning her
this way and that, in motion and repose.

Why am I not a poet? the painter writes.
But at least let me feel as much as possible

in each of my paintings, what I wish to produce
in the souls of others. He draws the dagger

from every angle but does not let her use it.
It's always the moment just before she kills.

III.

In some of the sketches she is pursued
by shadowy figures at the mouth of the cave—

in one a man is pressed against her back—
but in the formal study in oil, he paints

her and the boys alone, pursuers gone.
He captures her in flight, his brushstrokes wild,

all reds and golds but for a shadowy cape
flown off the mother's shoulders and hanging

there in an inky cloud behind her head.
It looks as though she is chased by herself.

IV.

By the Salon, the cape is gone and much
of the wildness. His *Furious Medea*

is composed, a study in stillness more horrifying
for its restraint: the tall isosceles

their bodies make, mother and sons conjoined
in an ironic Pietà, the beauty

of the mother's face, a single shadow fallen
across her brow to mark her fall from reason.

One feels deeply moved by this demented mother,
with her haggard eye, pale face, dry and livid mouth,

palpitating flesh, and burdened bosom,
a critic pens. The painter has expressed,

another writes, *a violent passion in*
its greatest energy and in all its truth.

V.

But the truth is there is no single truth—
even as others mass-market lithographs

of his creation, fixing her forever
in the public eye, Delacroix keeps trying

to get his vision right. Twenty years on,
he makes another with a different face.

Her gaze direct, more legibly conflicted,
this new Medea will be lost in war,

but she is lost to memory at once
as patrons pay to have her as she was.

So he fixes her to the canvas again, his true
Medea, adjusting his backgrounds, trimming

those monstrous limbs. Does he feel the limits tightening
as he paints? Creation and creator,

she clutches the dagger still, ever lovely,
ever ready to embrace or slit his throat.

Médée Furieuse, 1838

Furious Medea, Delacroix called her,
but I can see no rage, unless we count
her breasts, twin weapons pointing fiercely
at us, or the hand clenching a dagger,
its shadow slicing her nearest child's leg.
There is disorder in her hair and robes,
but her face, caught in profile, reveals what we
might read as sadness, a jaw too soft for anger.
The painting's tension lies in the lack of fury,
in the illusion that she might be guarding
the boys, in our knowledge that she is not.
And the children in her arms—they know it, too.
The one half-hugged, half-throttled squirms away.
The other is folded in a pose so close
to the surrender of nursing he seems at peace
almost, but for his eye, open wide—
and looking directly at us.
                          How many times
have I seen that look, the flash of fear
on my young daughter's face when I have raged
at her or some small thing? It passes, the fury
and the terror—my daughter puts on socks;
the driver yields—but I'm left shaken, a stranger.
Maybe all mothers murder their children's
innocence. In the painting, Medea holds
her boys so close they're one body again,
two cords she must cut. The children have no choice
but to love the hand that holds the knife.

The Swimmer

In the drawings, it takes a while for Delacroix
to settle on the children's resignation
as their mother marches them through a grotto

toward death. On canvas, their bodies will be limp,
even their squirms submissive, but in the center
of one sketch the larger child—he must be five

or six, not much older than my daughter—
has thrown one arm over Medea's shoulder,
as though he'd fight her off, or plead for love.

I think of that gesture, how fierce and futile,
as I stand shoulder-deep in pool water
days before my daughter learns to swim.

Her formal lessons forgotten, she grips my shoulder
the way the sketched boy clutches the mother
who holds the knife: as if I want to drown her

so she has to kill me first. She's thrashing wild
against the cage of my arms, holding on
as she pushes away, whimpering, now screaming.

The boy's arm is slender and straining, muscled
as a swimmer's, and I can't decide if my daughter's
right not to trust me, I who once cast her

from my body, who threaten and cajole,
who would in fact dunk her before she's ready.
Soon she'll learn to trust her body's buoyancy

and slide beneath the surface, unafraid,
but now she claws at me, pushing me under,
as though my arms weren't keeping her afloat.

Lay Figures

In his youth... Delacroix had many sessions with
female models devoted to activities other than posing.

—MARIE LATHERS, *Bodies of Art: French Literary
Realism and the Artist's Model*

I hadn't thought about those little men
in years, the wooden models cased in glass
at the art supply store, though I'd linger by them

after school, studying their blank faces
and jointed limbs, wondering what they were for
and who would buy them. Surprising then to find

their forms again in Delacroix's sketches,
to recognize in a master's hand the long O's
of their faces and torsos. In one series,

two mannequins instead of men lean in
to the mouth of a cave in the briefest of outlines,
while robed Medea is a maze of angles

and her dagger seems to tremble. Why wouldn't
the great artist rough out ideas by posing
figures who'd stay where they were put? Of course,

he might have drawn real men—what do I know
of artists' habits? But at a recent auction
a *mannequin d'atelier* sold from his studio,

and I was delighted to think that I was right
about the way he worked. He sketched live models,
too, and bedded many, but always finished

from the imagination, "unconstrained"
by the living features of man or girl. The figure
in the auction catalog was spindlier

than the ones I once admired, its knobby elbows
and fingers more expressive, somehow, though its face
just as empty—the way the artist must

have thought of the real girls too, mute and posable,
Interchangeable even, another set of tools.

On the Copy of a Rembrandt
Hung Beside Delacroix's Medea

Of course Medea dominates the room.
She towers, the one masterwork in a gallery
of minor Romantics, a whole wall to herself

but for the two tiny oils that flank her. One
makes sense—her own miniature, a roughed-out
likeness. The other, just as small, seems placed

for symmetry alone: an imitation
of Rembrandt's *Raphael Leaving the Family
of Tobias*—Delacroix must have seen

the original at the Louvre. Miracle
instead of madness, the angel, that one
luminous thing aloft, has healed the blind

and revealed himself. Tobit and Anna turn
away; their son and his new wife gaze up
at a wonder so small and poorly lit

most visitors walk past without pausing.
None of this is Delacroix's—the story,
the composition, the light, it's all received,

the good son powerless to do anything
but accept the stranger's gifts. Why hang it there,
in the shadow of that mythic mother,

who, if not the painter's own invention,
was transformed beneath his brush? Beside her,
of course the family doesn't stand a chance.

Poor Raphael, overlooked patron of travelers
and physicians, poor dutiful Tobias
and prostrate Tobit, poor helpless, wringing wives,

poor little dog lost to shadows trembling
on a chair in the sudden sight of light and goodness—
all are dwarfed beside that other, avenging angel

with her potions and her knife, as if to say
the miracle is that goodness ever wins.
—Or perhaps it is the other way around: that after

such large-scale fury, there must be some small
black frame with its single gleam consoling those
who stop to look, who need some consolation

no matter how diminutive, how much
the imitation pales compared to what
it tries and fails and tries to represent.

IV.

Still Life with Long-Range View

To return to the cabin you rented one long and happy weekend
      two years earlier is, of course, to find it diminished—
not in the way going back to some childhood landmark
      will shrink it to life-size, but an actual lessening:
the wooden bear you posed beside for photographs
      replaced by a smaller bear. Empty hooks where the hammock hung.

The fountain's still basin is clouded with larvae and home
      to three skittery frogs. Only the trees sloping
down the hill are greater now, their tops beginning to block
      the mountain view. And in the bushes by the porch,
something vast and moving, shifting against the leaves.

To return to a house you so briefly inhabited
      is to acknowledge your own diminishing. How could
you think it would be waiting, unchanged, for you alone?
      Try the view from every window, then try to tell yourself
the mountains in the distance will always be visible
      over the trees. That the creature in the undergrowth
is some small thing, casting a long shadow of sound.

The Undertow

The surface of the river briefly calm,
      our awkward strokes fallen into a rhythm
through luck if not talent, we could lift our eyes
      at last from our wobbling borrowed kayaks
and the water's snarling lip to scan the shore
      for the beauty our guide had promised us.
(The guide, impatient, had gone ahead.) And it
      was beautiful: quiet, green, and still
but for the vultures blotting out the trees,
      and then the death those hundreds of birds foretold.
The body of the deer was draped across the bank
      like a melting Dalí clock, the bloated bag
of the belly stretched to breaking. The hind legs
      dripped beneath the surface our paddles scraped.
My friends and I did not speak, not out of awe
      or because the scene brought us too close
to the great wordless beyond: our mouths were closed
      against the stench. The water we moved through,
that pooled in the bottoms of our flimsy crafts,
      all steeped in it. The vultures gathered and watched,
and did not feed. We paddled on, no faster
      than before, in search of our wayward guide
who'd be waiting near the rapids, and I forgot
      about that afternoon until this one,
when driving home from a friend's funeral
      I saw some black shape on the water as we crossed
a bridge. Who knows what I saw out the window,
      but in that flash of black, it all came back,
the hooded shapes, the white belly. I blinked,
      and whatever had caught my eye was gone again,
along with the rapids, the rocks, the chattering guide,
      the water that could pull us all under.

The Face in the Chalice

When my neighbor crosses the lawn between our houses
    brandishing the antlers of a freshly-killed buck,

red tissue still clinging to the nubs, and interrupts
    a family picnic, he can't know the mornings

my husband and I have stood by the window
    watching the sleeping deer beneath the trees,

their appearance ghostly, holy. He can't know
    that earlier this month a damaged man

opened fire in a warehouse, shooting seven,
    among them someone I once loved, whose life

hung between breath and mechanical breath,
    his eyes still opening, closing, crying, but empty,

or that I am raw with disbelief. In fact,
    our neighbor does not see me at all.

Breathless with joy, he describes his son's kill
    to my husband, who stands before my chair.

Watching the antlers in my neighbor's hands,
    trying not to scrutinize the pulpy flesh dangling,

I see what is not there as well as what is,
    the old optical illusion of the chalice become

two faces gazing. Would you say the soul
    left my friend when the bullet entered the body

and the brain emptied of oxygen, or when life support
    was pulled two weeks later? Minutes pass

before my neighbor notices me bent
    over the baby in my lap, still trying not to look.

He flushes as if to say he's sorry. The baby,
    focused only on my face, doesn't see a thing.

Elegy for City Life

How did we end up here, on this one-lane bridge
      with its flat brown rocks sliding always toward ruin,

easing our car past a rusted-out Oldsmobile
      on the bank of the creek below, a thin tree grown

through its empty windshield? In the summer it's swallowed by grass,
      a mystery emerging with the fall.

And this gray barn in the last stages of collapse,
      a small herd of cows still lining up at its troughs—

how have we come to pass it without wanting
      to photograph the caving roof, its rough,

calamitous beauty? How did our story
      place us here, in a rented house perched high

above the pasture, the lowing of the cows rising,
      troubling our dreams? Last week we heard

the bellowing all night. The next morning
      a black cow stood above a feeble calf

in a posture that looked like grief—we watched
      the mother's vigil, then the body alone

in the grass, the herd a distance away, and worried
      that no one would find the corpse, but by sunset

the grass was empty. How is it that some days
      the world seems shrunken, some days luminous and large

enough to praise the lone deer in the meadow,
    the hornet's globed nest gone dormant in our tree?

Praise Song

Some days, children jostle and poke
for the chance to feed the ragged goats
at the country trading post, the animals
toppling each other to be nearest
the hands that offer food. Usually,
though, it's just my daughter and me
and a cup of fifty-cent feed,
and the hens that circle our legs,
closing in as we toss corn and pellets,
and the owner scowling from the porch.
It should be beautiful to stand
this close to the natural world, our palms
stretched out, the tickling mouths working,
but most days when we drive by I lie
and tell my daughter the place is closed,
the goats are sleeping, though she can see
as well as I the kids standing
on the roof of their wooden shed. It's not
the filth, so much, that holds me back,
although it stinks in the summer,
but the animals' ruthlessness,
the way they thrust their heads through the gaps
in the fencing, fighting for space.
I reach for and fail the shy ones.

For proof the world is frightening,
look no further than the aggression
of goats and chickens, and children, too,
and even my own loathing, half-
understood, of the couple who run
this rickety petting zoo. Like us,
they clearly aren't from around here,
the woman blonde and tanned, country-

chic in designer overalls,
her fiancé a carpenter
with hair like Jesus. Last Easter, dressed
in a loincloth and a crown of thorns,
he tied himself to a cross outside
the store, and maybe I resent
the praise music booming from
the speakers and the showy faith
that brought them here, with no experience,
because they *prayed on it*. More likely,
though, I resent their falseness, the way
when no one's looking, they seem
to hate each other and the goats,
the woman radiating the kind
of disappointment I've taught myself
to hide, forcing myself to smile
at the smallness of our small-town lives
for my daughter's sake.
                        Or maybe
it's simpler than all that: the goats,
those virtuous pagans, remind me
too much of old men, crowded and penned
in some unkempt underworld where
no one's prayers will reach. Even the blind
black billy, his eyes sealed white
like a bearded Homer, the one
I'd like to think is—what?—absolved,
is driven by need to push and seek
and take the feed out of our hands.

At the Shore

This ruined castle slipping back to sand
is not a metaphor for our own ruin.
We're impermanent, of course. Yes, yes,

we are frail. But this castle, set back from the shore,
is victim to neither time nor tide. No,
a child, my child, stands over it, dousing it

with seawater, toppling the turrets
of her masterpiece with buckets of wet sand,
creating, destroying in one motion,

the way the stick she found in the waves (a piece
of seagrass, really) returned to her feet,
surprising her, when she dropped it in the water.

She followed the same script each time: *my stick,*
I dropped my stick. I miss my stick… My stick!
I don't understand waves, the pull and return,

much better; I was stumped in high school science
by the diagrams of corks bobbing in place,
the teacher's claim that the water didn't move,

only the energy surging through it did,
when anyone could see the seaweed piled
on the beach. All those conflicting forces.

I walk behind my daughter now, feeling
stupid and grateful as she drops her pail
and turns her attention to the task of writing

her name. The castle long abandoned, its towers
a melted cake, she spells the letters I carve,
kicking at the waves when our work is washed away.

Shocks and Changes

Summoned at 3, I soothe my daughter's cries
and, turning back toward bed, turn off her light.
Out of the dark, a galaxy appears,
pale stars scattered across the plaster skies
by some other child who thought this room at night
would be his always. The moons, the meteors—
all his hours spent peeling and arranging—
for two years now have hung above my head
entirely unnoticed. The old wives' tale
says all the stars whose light we see are dead,
but that's not true. We fail to see them changing
as they change. And on this closer, human scale
and present tense, this room, this child I've kissed,
this night will always and never quite exist.

On Domesticity

Around a blind corner, a shape in the road,
    dark and crouching, regards my car a half-

moment then sprints up the hill into the woods
    beside our house where my husband works inside.

It's not until it darts that I can name it,
    bobcat, that rumor that's haunted our neighborhood,

such as it is, for the last year, a specter
    picking off the groundhogs and feral cats.

I call Jim, breathless with what I've seen,
    and he rushes outside toward the danger,

which of course is gone. We are not mountain people—
    we do not hike or camp or commune with these woods

and how we came to live among others' second homes
    still baffles us—but these glimpses of the wild,

fleeting, vicarious, let us feel something
    more than our usual ennui, that vague

longing for the city and restaurants and lights
    that keeps us from feeling at home, and so we listen

for the clicks and howls of the unnamed in the dark,
    we look for the moving shadows beyond our lawn

perhaps because we know how much our own
    wildness has been tamed. I remember the fights

we used to have, how I'd collapse in tears,
        how gingerly we would touch each other

when we were ready to touch. And then we married
        and had a child, and there was no point to it,

to shaking the calm for the thrill of being right.
        What wild things are left are in our books:

Our daughter has us roar and shake our claws
        so she can say BE STILL! and silence us.

On Reading Maurice Sendak
Instead of Anaïs Nin

I wanted to write a poem about sex,
the sex of the long-married, about desire,
its departures and returns, by way of the bobcat
I met by chance on the curving lane below
our house—it bolted, I drove on. Its body,
the surprise of it—and my husband's body,
his muscular hide sleek as an animal's,
which after all this time should not surprise

but does. I tried to write the poem praising
my husband's form, the poem of gratitude,
joy even—I'll use that word—but a phrase
from a book intruded, a children's book, followed
by an actual child, our daughter dropping
her towel, shouting *Nay-Nay!* and darting away,
and it was her bright, joyful body I followed,
laughing, out of the poem and the room.

Story Time

My daughter wants to read the book about the bears
who go to camp, piling each day onto a bus
driven by the jovial director, Grizzly Bob.
Despite the joys of arts & crafts and relay races,
one cub spends all summer dreading the last night,
when the campers climb Spook Hill to sleep under the stars.
In picture-book logic, everything turns out fine,
but my daughter says she'd want me there to keep her safe,
and I can't help but think of one of the oldest stories
I know, the one where my father's sent to summer camp,
and while he's gone his family moves away.
                                          The day
it ends and the camp bus drops him at the curb, he rings
the bell on vacant rooms. My father's just a boy,
in third or fourth grade, and he has no key, so he sits
on the porch and waits, and eventually his parents sidle up,
laughing at the joke he wasn't in on. Because
this is no picture book, there's no joyous reunion,
no tears and repentance, no moralizing lesson,
and the shadows that look like monsters turn out to be
not the shadows of chairs or coatracks, but monsters' shadows.
He laughs now when he tells the story, which usually
begins, *You think your childhood was bad...*
                                          To joke
is to make light of the heavy burdens, the bruises,
the boxes my father did not pack, when someone else
sorted the little he must have had that was his.
My daughter's sleep is broken by dreams she can't describe,
but before she calls for me, I'm there, patting her arm,
our voices making light of, easing back the dark.
On the last night of bear camp, Grizzly Bob tells stories
so wondrous no one can be scared. I imagine that my father,

years before he would become my father, not knowing what they'd done this time, still knew enough to dread the final night of camp because it was the last.

Chemistry Lessons

The glass thermometer shattered,
mercury sliding across the tile,

my mother knelt in the spilt silver
discarding shards of glass, chasing

the freed beads onto a plate.
Once she'd caught them all, she called me

to see how the mercury rolled
and roiled, the big beads swallowing

the small, then shivering apart
at the shake of the plate. I watched

them gather and quake. I'd swear I played
all afternoon, poking the beads

shiny as joy, in love with the gleam
and with my mother. And she in turn

remembers summer afternoons
when, as a child, she went running

behind mosquito trucks, joining
the children up and down the street

skipping through the great white clouds
of poison. And I wonder what dangers

I'll offer my daughter as distraction
when the hours till bedtime swell,

and whether she, having survived
those dangers, remembering them someday

will insist that they were beautiful.

In the Shower, My Daughter Studies My Naked Form

Her hair shampooed and rinsed, her eyes safe now
to open, my daughter gazes on my body
while I fight the urge to turn away. How hard
it is to be held in the eyes of another.

I used to pose for artists, hopeful one
might find me beautiful and teach me how,
but as they sketched I looked out the window
or over their heads, afraid to meet their eyes

or see myself as I'd been rendered.
They weren't looking at me exactly, but
at shapes and shadows, at intersecting planes,
an invention in an invented room.

My daughter looks more closely than a painter.
She rubs my ruined belly, pokes my hips.
Soaping my knees with her small hands, she studies me
the way I've stood before a work of art,

examining those diaphanous bathers
or some Dutch still life, lemons and fish
on a platter, the ordinary gleaming,
or the way I stand and watch her as she sleeps.

Self-Portrait in Wood or Stone or Air

I imagine that I still exist
in replicate, an artifact,

if inexact, of afternoons
spent naked on an artist's couch.

I posed, she drew. Self and not-self,
impression and not fact, somewhere

I may be carved in wood or wax
or cast in bronze or chiseled out

of stone, my face, my hips, my lips
refracted through another pair

of eyes and hands. I saw only
sketches, not what she made of them,

so I can only imagine myself
smaller or larger than life, standing

in a corner realistic or abstract
or curved upon a table, avoiding

or embracing some viewer's gaze,
lovelier surely than I was

at twenty when I posed, unable
to see myself in any future.

And now, searching for the artist,
I learn that I'm a year too late,

finding her obit instead
of what she sculpted.

               —What would console

the girl I was or would become?
Not the tributes to the dead

but my own insistence that I did
not land, all knees, in some lost drawer,

but am here and there, in fact, in form.

NOTES

The italicized lines in "Introduction to Patriarchy" quote *Playboy's* December 1984 Playmate Questionnaire.

The section titles of "Introduction to Art History" refer, respectively, to Marcel Duchamp's urinal turned on its side, signed R. Mott, and christened *Fountain;* to an imaginary lecture; and to Sandro Botticelli's *Birth of Venus.*

The poems in Part III are inspired by and in conversation with Eugene Delacroix's painting *Médée Furieuse,* first exhibited in Paris in 1838, as well as a series of thirty-one sketches and a formal study in oil, all of which are part of the permanent collection of the Palais des Beaux Arts in Lille, France.

"On the Copy of a Rembrandt Hung Beside Delacroix's Medea" refers to the painting *L'Ange Raphael Quittant Tobie.* The copy is attributed to Delacroix, though its authorship is unproven.

Amanita phalloides is the scientific name of the death cap mushroom.

"Shocks and Changes" owes its title to Robert Frost's "On Looking Up by Chance at the Constellations."

Poems in Part IV allude to *Where the Wild Things Are,* by Maurice Sendak, and *The Berenstain Bears Go to Camp,* by Stan and Jan Berenstain.

"Self Portrait in Wood or Stone or Air" remembers the artist Holly Jill Smith, 1969–2014.

ACKNOWLEDGMENTS

Grateful acknowledgment is made to the editors of the following journals in which some of these poems first appeared:

32 Poems: "Introduction to Desire"; *Birmingham Poetry Review:* "The Corinthian Women" and "In the Shower My Daughter Studies My Naked Form"; *Cincinnati Review:* "Still Life with Long-Range View"; *Five Points:* "Introduction to Home Economics" and "Introduction to Vigilance"; *Great River Review:* "Metamorphoses," "Self-Portrait in Wood or Stone or Air," and "The Stitch"; *Hopkins Review:* "Shocks and Changes"; *Literary Matters:* "Chemistry Lessons, "Incompetent Cervix," and "Lay Figures"; *Missouri Review:* "The Face in the Chalice," "Introduction to Art History," "Introduction to Patriarchy," "Introduction to Sex Education," "Postpartum: A Fairy Tale," and "The Swimmer"; *Pleiades:* "On the Copy of a Rembrandt Hung Beside Delacroix's Medea"; *Plume:* "Praise Song"; *Southern Review: "Médée Furieuse, 1838"; *StorySouth:* "Introduction to Gerontology"; *Talking River:* "Elegy for City Life" and "The Undertow"; *Terminus:* "Introduction to Captivity," "Introduction to Thanatology," "On Domesticity," and "On Reading Maurice Sendak Instead of Anaïs Nin"; *Virginia Quarterly Review:* "Introduction to Statistics."

Thanks to the Academy of American Poets for featuring "Introduction to Mycology" in its Poem-a-Day series.

I am grateful to Young Harris College and the Sewanee Writers' Conference for their encouragement and support. I'm also grateful to Lauren Watel for her generous reading of these poems and to MaryKatherine Callaway and the incredible team at LSU press for bringing the book to life.

Special thanks to the staff of the Palais des Beaux Arts in Lille, France, for providing me access to the sketches and documentation for Eugene Delacroix's *Médée Furieuse*. Thanks, too, to my colleague Claudie Massicotte who assisted with translations of my correspondence into and out of French, and to the art historian Dorothy Johnson, both for her highly informative book *David to Delacroix: The Rise of Romantic Mythology* and her willingness to answer questions from a stranger.

Thanks to my mother for bearing me, bearing with me, and reading these poems with love and good humor.

My eternal gratitude to the late Claudia Emerson, who saw and believed in the earliest version of this manuscript. And to Jim May, always my first and best reader.